Anderson Public Library
114 N. Main
Lawrenceburg, KY 40342

Word Play

Punctuation
at the Game

By Kathleen Connors

Gareth Stevens
Publishing

Please visit our website, www.garethstevens.com. For a free color catalog of all our high-quality books, call toll free 1-800-542-2595 or fax 1-877-542-2596.

Library of Congress Cataloging-in-Publication Data

Connors, Kathleen.
Punctuation at the game / Kathleen Connors.
    p. cm. — (Word play)
Includes index.
ISBN 978-1-4339-7196-9 (pbk.)
ISBN 978-1-4339-7197-6 (6-pack)
ISBN 978-1-4339-7195-2 (library binding)
1. English language—Punctuation—Juvenile literature. I. Title.
PE1450.C76 2012
428.2'3—dc23
                                            2011052711

First Edition

Published in 2013 by
Gareth Stevens Publishing
111 East 14th Street, Suite 349
New York, NY 10003

Copyright © 2013 Gareth Stevens Publishing

Designer: Ben Gardner
Editor: Kristen Rajczak

Photo credits: Cover, p. 1 © iStockphoto.com/Sean Locke; p. 5 © iStockphoto.com/Andrew Rich; p. 7 © iStockphoto.com/Terry J. Alcorn; p. 9 Lane V. Erickson/Shutterstock.com; p. 11 Fotokostic/Shutterstock.com; p. 13 © iStockphoto.com/Steve Debenport; p. 15 © iStockphoto.com/Colleen Butler; p. 17 Suzanne Tucker/Shutterstock.com; p. 19 Juriah Mosin/Shutterstock.com.

All rights reserved. No part of this book may be reproduced in any form without permission in writing from the publisher, except by a reviewer.

Printed in the United States of America

CPSIA compliance information: Batch #CS12GS: For further information contact Gareth Stevens, New York, New York at 1-800-542-2595.

Contents

Play Ball! 4

Great Game 6

Using Periods. 8

Exclamation Points. 10

Get Excited! 12

Just Ask 14

So Many Sports 16

Speed Up with Colons. 18

Cool Commas 20

Glossary. 22

For More Information. 23

Index 24

Boldface words appear in the glossary.

Play Ball!

Do you like to play sports or watch them on TV? Let's learn about some different kinds with the help of some punctuation marks.

Punctuation is the name for the group of marks that make sentences easier to read.

Great Game

Baseball is called America's **pastime**. People of all ages like to play.

What's the dot at the end of the sentence? That's a period. Periods show the end of the kind of sentence called a statement. Statements often report facts.

Using Periods

Baseball games have nine innings. Other sports games are broken into halves or quarters. These sentences state facts. A period is used to show when each sentence ends.

Exclamation Points

It's so much fun to win a game. It's even better when you've made the winning play! An exclamation point is another punctuation mark that's used to end a sentence. It's used to show strong feelings, such as anger or excitement.

11

Get Excited!

Goal! Your team might call this out when you score a point in soccer or hockey. They're happy for you!

An exclamation point can show when something is shouted out, or exclaimed.

Just Ask

What's the score? Check the **scoreboard**! It's important to know whether your team is winning or losing.

Question marks go at the end of a sentence that asks a question.

So Many Sports

There are so many sports to choose from. What's your favorite? Do you like bowling, swimming, or gymnastics?

These sentences end with a question mark to show they're questions.

Speed Up with Colons

Scoreboards show time left in a game or how fast a runner is. If there are 5 minutes and 25 seconds left, the scoreboard will read 05:25.

Colons are punctuation marks used to show time. They also come before lists and explanations.

Cool Commas

Playing football is a lot of fun. To score points, you have to catch, throw, and run with your team!

Commas are another common punctuation mark. Use a comma to show separation between words or groups of words in a sentence or list.

Common Punctuation Marks

name	mark	when to use
period	.	ends a sentence that is a statement
exclamation point	!	ends a sentence that shows strong feelings
question mark	?	ends a sentence that asks a question
colon	:	helps show time, comes before a list or explanation
comma	,	shows separation between words or groups of words

Glossary

pastime: an activity that someone enjoys during their free time

scoreboard: a large board that shows the score and time in a game or race

For More Information

Books

Ganeri, Anita. *Punctuation: Commas, Periods, and Question Marks.* Chicago, IL: Heinemann Library, 2011.

Heinrichs, Ann. *Punctuation.* Mankato, MN: Child's World, 2011.

Websites

Punctuation Games for Kids
www.funenglishgames.com/grammargames/punctuation.html
Practice placing punctuation marks in this game.

Punctuation Rap
www.NationalPunctuationDay.com/playtimerap.html
Read the words and listen to this rap about punctuation.

Publisher's note to educators and parents: Our editors have carefully reviewed these websites to ensure that they are suitable for students. Many websites change frequently, however, and we cannot guarantee that a site's future contents will continue to meet our high standards of quality and educational value. Be advised that students should be closely supervised whenever they access the Internet.

Index

baseball 6, 8
bowling 16
colons 18, 21
commas 20, 21
exclamation point 10, 12, 21
explanations 18, 21
facts 6, 8
football 20
games 8, 10
groups of words 20, 21
hockey 12
lists 18, 20, 21
marks 4, 10, 18, 20, 21

soccer 12
periods 6, 8, 21
question 14, 16, 21
question mark 14, 16, 21
score 12, 14, 20
scoreboard 14, 18
shout 12
sports 4, 16
statements 6, 21
strong feelings 10, 21
swimming 16
time 18, 21
words 20, 21

Anderson Public Library
114 N. Main
Lawrenceburg, KY 40342